newborn
YOUR

promise
PROJECT

GROUP STUDY

YOUR
newborn
promise
PROJECT

GROUP STUDY

CALLIE GRANT, AUDRA HANEY, AND CHARISSA KOLAR

Graham
Blanchard

Austin, Texas

Your Newborn Promise Project Group Study

http://www.grahamblanchard.com

Library of Congress Cataloging-in-Publication Data in Progress

Cover Design & Illustrations: Missi Jay

Interior Book Design: Suzanne Lawing

Printed in the United States of America

1 2 3 4 5 6 7 8 9 10

TABLE OF CONTENTS

Introduction
A Newborn
Promise for All

W elcome to *Your Newborn Promise Project Group Study*, a time for expecting and new parents to plan for big life change. The arrival of a child is a watershed event, a spiritual passage of life for infants and parents alike. God brings a child into the world already primed to know and to grow in him (Ecclesiastes 3:11, Romans 1:20). At the same time, new parents enter an entirely new phase in marriage and personal growth. This confluence of transitions is like a gift from God to bring us closer to him and to each other.

You might be exploring faith after many years of drifting from God, and now on the parenting threshold are thinking earnestly about him for the first time in a long time. Maybe you never knew him, but find yourself more curious about him than before. Or, perhaps your soul, already long connected with Jesus, is now stirred by other unnamed yearnings for your new child.

For these six sessions, invest yourself in being here, contributing to the discussion, and reflecting with others. As a couple and individually, your task is to spiritually assess and plan for your exciting new parenting role, while permitting God to beneficially heal and transform you along the way. This is *your* newborn promise project. God spiritually fits you for the task, as you apply your God-given abilities to *love, remember, seek, question,* and *persevere.* Along the way, you will see how the Bible urges you, over and over again, to use these spiritual abilities.

There may never be a better time. When planning for a family, a common desire is to make a better life for our children than we had, to not repeat the harm or mistakes of our past, to carry forward treasured experiences from our childhood and make them even better, if possible. God himself inspires such desire in those who put their faith in him. He is the God of transformation: "I will give you a new heart and put a new spirit in you; I will remove from you your heart of stone and give you a heart of flesh" (Ezekiel 36:26). To do so, the loving Father sent his Son. In this study, Jesus will be our way, our truth, and our life (John 14:6).

Your group work complements *Your Newborn Promise Project: A Christian Pre-Parenting Primer for Husband and Wife.* The group sessions align with chapters in the primer, which we encourage you to read for your individual benefit. The primer also gives five Bible-based newborn facts of life, as well as Learn, Absorb, Praise, and Connect activities for you to intimately plan for the spiritual development of the whole family.

Your child's spiritual formation will take place in much the same way, as together you learn, absorb, praise, and connect in the settings of family life and community. Reading to your child from birth is vital for your child's cognitive and emotional development, and it is a primary gateway for spiritual formation. In each session, you will have the opportunity to read related board books. The Learn, Absorb & Praise™ collection forms your child's first curriculum for developing Christ-likeness. This is *your newborn's* newborn promise project.

Let's not delay! Bring out your Bibles and expect God to work wonders in your new life together.

Session One
Now What?

He has made everything beautiful in its time. He has also set eternity in the human heart; yet no one can fathom what God has done from beginning to end.

—ECCLESIASTES 3:11

Opening Prayer

Thank God for bringing you together and ask him to create lasting ties as you reflect on his unfathomable creations.

Video Introduction

Video #1 – The beauty, potential, and sometimes humorous hazards of your newborn promise.

Session Objective

One of the first thoughts couples often have when bringing home their new child is "Now what do we do?" They sense the immensity of the moment, and have no idea where it will take them or whether they are fully prepared. Together, we will explore what God has in store during this important life change.

Small Group Discussion

Break into your small groups for the next three discussion topics designed to bring you closer together and prepare for the remaining weeks ahead.

1. Share your baby story

For you created my inmost being; you knit me together in my mother's womb. I praise you because I am fearfully and wonderfully made; your works are wonderful, I know that full well.

—PSALM 139:13-14

> New parenthood is a great leveler of any superficial differences you might have with others in your group or class, but your journeys here took many paths.

Welcome to parenthood! You all are starting from the same ground zero in unknown territory. However, your journey getting here was unique. Take some time to get to know one another in this session, first by sharing your baby story.

Go around the group, introduce yourselves, each spouse taking turns, and answer questions like these:

- Where are you from? How did you meet your spouse?

- Why do you want to be parents?

- What options for growing your family were you considering and why?

- Have you had any physical or spiritual challenges in becoming a parent?

_____

_____

_____

_____

_____

_____

_____

_____

_____

_____

_____

_____

_____

"This world, after all our science and sciences, is still a miracle; wonderful, inscrutable, magical, and more, to whosoever will think of it."

—Thomas Carlyle

2. Admire God's creation

For we are God's handiwork, created in Christ Jesus to do good works, which God prepared in advance for us to do.

—EPHESIANS 2:10

> Childbirth might be an everyday and common event, but it still is an extraordinary happening. Pause to take a collective deep breath, gather your thoughts, and simply admire the amazing miracles that are now unfolding in your presence.

Never has there been, nor will there be again, a child or a family like yours. You have a destiny (Psalm 139:16). The journey into this new, unexplored world of your child and your family life will be guided by the wisdom of the Bible, experience throughout the ages, and the latest research, which confirms the great miracle you all are.

God chose you, at this place and time, to be part of his creative, redemptive, love-filled work. Take turns discussing the possibilities with these questions as your guide:

- How has God amazed you in this new life?
- What do you look forward to most about your growing family?
- In what ways do you feel ready or not?
- How is this season affecting your faith?

- What are some funny things that happened to you along the way?

_____

_____

_____

_____

_____

_____

_____

_____

_____

_____

_____

_____

_____

_____

_____

_____

_____

_____

_____

_____

_____

_____

3. Commit to renewal

"How can someone be born when they are old?" Nicodemus asked. "Surely they cannot enter a second time into their mother's womb to be born!"

Jesus answered, "Very truly I tell you, no one can enter the kingdom of God unless they are born of water and the Spirit. Flesh gives birth to flesh, but Spirit gives birth to spirit."

—JOHN 3:4-6

> The life transition you are going through holds great promise for spiritual rebirth and growth. This is your whole family's newborn promise. Determine as a husband and wife, and as a small group, to embrace it.

As you carefully plan for the physical needs of your child, this season of transitions and "firsts" calls especially for the care of spiritual needs, too, for the benefit of the entire family. Bringing a new child home is a seismic shift in life that changes everything. The invitation to embrace the transition with God's grace and mercy is truly the opportunity of a lifetime.

Read John 3 aloud in your group and then discuss the passage with these questions:

- Why does Jesus teach that we must be born again?

- How can a grown person be born again?
- What promises does God make in John 3?

"Therefore, if anyone is in Christ, the new creation has come: The old has gone, the new is here!"
—2 Corinthians 5:17

_____

_____

_____

_____

_____

_____

_____

_____

_____

_____

_____

_____

_____

_____

_____

Small Group Wrap-Up

Close your small group time by sharing any concerns or prayer requests and commit to praying over them in the upcoming week.

Session Recap

- If in a class, reconvene in the large group. Choose one group or a participant to recap the session highlights.
- The opening passage for this session states that God has "made everything beautiful in its time." The infinite variety of humanity and the rest of God's creation attest to his great power and his benevolence for all he has made.

My takeaways from this session:

_____

_____

_____

_____

_____

_____

_____

_____

_____

_____

_____

_____

This Week at Home

Have a date night with your spouse and read your wedding vows to each other. Talk about the reasons you got married and what the biggest challenges have been. If you haven't yet, read the Introduction: A Newborn Promise for All, in order to be grounded in the goals of your time here. Pray about your future together as a family, and ask God to help you understand the importance of being born again.

Next Steps

In the next five sessions, you will find two board book connections from the Learn, Absorb & Praise™ children's collection (see Helpful Resources). Consider choosing one to read aloud as you close your time together. It will reinforce the topics you cover and remind you why you are doing this spiritual assessment and planning. When reading the board books, anticipate the pleasure of cuddling with your baby, while sharing God's wonders and words.

Closing Prayer

Close your group time in prayer, thanking God for the opportunity to freely meet and seek his plans for your family and your future together.

Session Two

Love

Place me like a seal over your heart,
like a seal on your arm;
for love is as strong as death,
its jealousy unyielding as the grave.
It burns like blazing fire,
like a mighty flame.
Many waters cannot quench love;
rivers cannot sweep it away.

—SONG OF SONGS 8:6-7

Opening Prayer

Ask God for wisdom, guidance, and insight into understanding his meaning of Love.

Video Introduction

Video #2 – The spiritual power of love and the true bond that it forges.

Session Objective

Because we are created in God's image, love creates a spiritual bond, not a physical one. Marriages and families are primarily spiritual unions of love. The Bible depicts love best. Let's look closely at what God says about love.

Small Group Discussion

Break into your small groups for the next three discussion topics designed to help you understand God's view of love and the spiritual quality of it.

1. Examine the human anatomy

One of the teachers of the law came and heard them debating. Noticing that Jesus had given them a good answer, he asked him, "Of all the commandments, which is the most important?"

"The most important one," answered Jesus, "is this: 'Hear, O Israel: The Lord our God, the Lord is one. Love the Lord your God with all your heart and with all your soul and with all your mind and with all your strength.' The second is this: 'Love your neighbor as yourself.' There is no commandment greater than these."

—MARK 12:28-31

Loving God wholly with all my heart, mind, strength, and soul—my whole being—is the basis of my faith, and is foundational for loving my spouse and raising our new child.

In Jewish and then Christian tradition the terms *spirit, heart,* and *soul* are used to describe the unseen life of a person. The meanings of these terms have been diluted and distorted over time by their broad use in society. But true meanings matter, because philosophies, parenting styles, and daily choices grow out of them.

Your will is in essence your *spirit*. As your decision maker, your will resides at the very *heart* or core of who you are. Your *soul* encompasses all aspects of your being—your thoughts, emotions, decisions, actions, and beliefs.

The beliefs and decisions of the will direct a person's life. It's what makes you who you are. But it is not the strongest component of your being, yet. You only begin to realize its potential and power when God is one with you there. And that requires your permission.

Christians of all backgrounds—Catholic, Orthodox, and Protestant—hold that the first step of faith is for a person to decide, with a turning of the will, to believe in God. "If you confess with your mouth that Jesus is Lord and believe in your heart that God raised him from the dead, you will be saved. For with the heart one believes and is justified, and with the mouth one confesses and is saved" (Romans 10:9-10, ESV).

The heart, then, serves as the seat of faith and love—the home of the spirit, the place where decisions and beliefs guide the entire life: "Above all else, guard your heart, for everything you do flows from it" (Proverbs 4:23). As such, people are, above all, primarily spiritual beings. Whether you view your child as a primarily spiritual or physical being will guide your parenting journey.

- Read aloud Mark 12:28-31 and reflect on each command. Why do you think God commands us to first love him?

- Why do you think Jesus names the several aspects of a person to be applied to loving God?

- How does love affect you spiritually?

- If our souls were visible on the outside of us, we would probably take better care of them. What would yours look like? How would you care for it differently? Or your child's? See what the Bible says about "clothing" the soul in Romans 13:14 and Colossians 3:12.

_____

_____

_____

_____

2. Set your heart on devotion

As the Father has loved me, so have I loved you. Now remain in my love. If you keep my commands, you will remain in my love, just as I have kept my Father's commands and remain in his love. I have told you this so that my joy may be in you and that your joy may be complete. My command is this: Love each other as I have loved you.

— JOHN 15:9-12

Love for God and family starts with willful commitment, and it grows through good times and bad, under God's loving care.

Growing love is never an accident. It is the result of a heart's bent, and a willful decision to choose love and oneness over hate and division. If people "fall out of love" it is because they choose to out of pride, selfishness, or indifference. It can be a painfully easy choice or drift.

On the other hand, if you devote yourself to choosing love and fostering its growth, then God and all the forces of Heaven are aligned to help you. Miraculously, simply praying for your love to grow opens up the potential to make it so (Philippians 1:9, 1 Thessalonians 3:12).

- Describe another area of your life where you set your heart on devotion by investing significant time or energy and experienced a tangible result.

- How do you think culture views a wedding ceremony—as the starting point or as the climax of love? How does either perspective impact a marriage?

- In John 15:9-12, what does Jesus say about love?

"The colored sunsets
and the starry heavens,
the beautiful mountains
and the shining seas,
the fragrant woods and
the painted flowers are
not half so beautiful as a
soul who is serving Jesus
out of love, in the wear
and tear of common,
unpoetic life."
—Frederick William Faber,
All for Jesus

3. Know love's greatest strength

Greater love has no one than this:
to lay down one's life for one's friends.
—JOHN 15:13

When you devote yourself to loving God, he uses your acts of service and sacrifice to unlock your self-absorption and transform you. Service and sacrifice are profoundly spiritual acts using emotional and physical energy to magnify love and bond us in marriage and family.

Just as God's physical laws manage outcomes in the physical world, so it is with life in the spiritual world. A profoundly mysterious truth of God's order is that service and sacrifice not only magnify love, but they also grow it. Marriage and parenthood offer ideal circumstances to experience the heights of love.

- Read aloud the parable of the Good Samaritan in Luke 10:25-37. Who is the neighbor in the story and why?

- Share times in your life that your love has grown when you served or sacrificed.

- In 1 Corinthians 13, Paul writes that "love never fails." How has unfailing love been apparent in your marriage so far? How do you expect it to be true with your child?

_____

_____

_____

_____

_____

_____

_____

_____

_____

_____

_____

_____

_____

_____

_____

_____

_____

Small Group Wrap-Up

Close your small group time by sharing answered prayers over the past week. Share new concerns or prayer requests and commit to praying over them in the upcoming week.

Session Recap

- If in a class, reconvene in the large group. Choose one group or a participant to recap the session highlights.

- The opening passage for this session states that "love is stronger than death." The love Jesus displayed on the cross is the ultimate fulfillment of this passage because he defeated death and lives in us today.

- Share experiences from the Session 1 "This Week at Home," having a date night to revisit your wedding vows.

My takeaways from this session:

_____

_____

_____

_____

_____

_____

_____

_____

_____

_____

_____

_____

This Week at Home

As you anticipate the arrival of your baby or if you already have your bundle at home, you likely feel so many wonderful emotions. Spend time before the next session reflecting on love and bending your will to it intentionally in trying circumstances. Pray for God to grow your love for those you perceive as unlovable.

In light of your study time, extend the lesson to prepare for loving your child in God's strength and wisdom. Write a letter to your child expressing your hopes for the kind of parent you will be, making a commitment to nourish your child with unconditional love, and asking for forgiveness for mistakes you will make along the way. Going back and reading it at various stages in your child's life will remind you about your hopes and keep you on course. When the time is right, you can pass on this family heirloom to your child.

Next Steps

- Discuss logistics related to the next time you'll meet.
- Read aloud one of the early childhood board book connections:
  Jesus Shows Me, The Knowing My God Series
  Your Core

Closing Prayer

Close your group time in prayer, asking God to grow your love this week by helping you bear with one another, serve one another, and build up one another.

Session Three
Remember

Praise the LORD, O my soul;
  all my inmost being, praise his holy name.
Praise the LORD O my soul,
  and forget not his benefits—
who forgives all your sins
  and heals all your diseases,
who redeems your life from the pit
  and crowns you with love and compassion,
who satisfies your desires with good things
  so your youth is renewed like the eagle's.

—PSALM 103:1-5

Opening Prayer

Ask God to help you take to heart his vital guidance about remembering.

Video Introduction

Video #3 – The spiritual lifeline of remembering recalls and reveals our life with God.

Session Objective

This new phase in your life, as future-oriented as it tends to be, must be truthfully informed by the past and healthfully rooted in it. Time—history—is a friend to faith. In fact, having a child-like faith, which pleases Jesus, requires continually remembering how God has revealed himself in human history and in our lives personally.

Small Group Discussion

Break into your small groups for the next three discussion topics designed to explore the beneficial role of actively remembering in personal and family faith.

1. Re-parent your soul

When [Jesus] saw the crowds, he had compassion on them, because they were harassed and helpless, like sheep without a shepherd.

—MATTHEW 9:36

Whatever the scope of your memories, remembering helps you identify and name previous facts and feelings, put them in their proper place, and decide how they will inform your life today and tomorrow.

Everything new you learn and decide about parenting now can be applied to the child you once were, and in a way, permit you to re-parent your soul. In fact, as an adult, you are now responsible for the child you once were. Did you have an aloof parent? Well, here you are now holding your child and deciding, "that won't happen here anymore."

In the Christian faith, the past does not bog us down. Every day is new. "Because of the Lord's great love we are not consumed, for his compassions never fail. They are new every morning; great is your faithfulness" (Lamentations 3:22-23).

Can God build upon your positive memories and transform the hard and ugly ones into something beautiful for your family? You bet he can. Thousands of years of human experience with a very personal God testify to it. Remember: He "heals the brokenhearted and binds up their wounds" (Psalm 147:30). Those words were written by one who knew.

- Identify a few areas where re-parenting your soul could be helpful (such as by showing love or appropriate discipline, being truthful, establishing healthy routines). What will you do differently?
- Stepping back and getting perspective on the tender mercies and kindnesses in your life can strengthen renewal and restore hope. Tell of one or two specific times as a child that you knew God was with you.

Examining family history can be very painful and unearth memories or feelings that need to be processed with a professional counselor. Contact your church or family doctor for referrals, and know that any steps you take toward healing will benefit all of your significant relationships.

2. Survey your spiritual roots

And I pray that you, being rooted and established in love, may have the power, together with all the Lord's holy people, to grasp how wide and long and high and deep is the love of Christ, and to know this love, which surpasses knowledge—that you may be filled to the measure of all the fullness of God.

—EPHESIANS 3:17-19

Our first impressions of God come from our family of origin. But we have deep spiritual roots that go back thousands of years—all Christians do. We benefit when we remember them.

As Christians, we are firmly rooted in the ideas, teaching, traditions, hopes, and love of God's chosen people, now as his chosen people, too. We do well to stay connected with that history, while examining our own and remembering God's part in it all.

Some people identify closely with their family of origin, while others have very few family ties. Regardless, the idea of "rootlessness" should be a foreign concept to a Christian, who has been grafted into the family of God through the work of Jesus (John 15:1-8, Romans 11:11-24). With him, we are rooted and established forever in love.

- What was your first impression about God that your family of origin gave to you?

- Read aloud Ephesians 3:1-6. Since we are rooted in the family of God, the Bible can be viewed as an account of our spiritual ancestors. Name a happening in the Bible that involves a person with whom you identify and why.

- How have Christian friends or your church provided the benefits of family? What do you do to help build and grow your Christian relationships?

3. Remember not to forget

The Spirit of the Lord is on me, because he has anointed me to proclaim good news to the poor. He has sent me to proclaim freedom for the prisoners and recovery of sight for the blind, to set the oppressed free, to proclaim the year of the Lord's favor.

—Luke 4:18-19

> We carry a habit of willful forgetting into adulthood because it often achieves our goal. Willful forgetting allows a person to slide by focusing on external or superficial matters, while neglecting the condition of the true inner self.

Works in progress that we are, we all have seasons of being stubborn and prideful in our dealings with God, forgetting to revere, obey, and love Him. But willful forgetting is the easiest way for life to run off the rails. It is detrimental to the inner condition and permits wrong-doing—big and small—as people push thoughts of God out of their minds and ignore him.

The cost of forgetting or even passively drifting away in faith through neglect is high, and far too easy to do with the many physical distractions in this life. But God helps us. In Luke 4 quoted above, Jesus proclaimed his purpose on earth. At the last meal before He went to the cross to fulfill it, Jesus instituted a new sacrament, the Holy Communion, to help us remember what he did (Luke 22:19).

- Open your Bible to Jesus' parable of the Prodigal Son in Luke 15. What did the main character forget? What jarred his memory? Do you see yourself in this parable?

- Over and over again, the Bible stresses remembering and not forgetting. Use your Bible concordance to choose a few passages and read them aloud to discuss the results of forgetting.

- What spiritually healthy habits help you combat forgetting about God and nurture your family's faith?

_____

_____

_____

_____

_____

_____

_____

_____

_____

_____

_____

_____

Small Group Wrap-Up

Close your small group time by sharing answered prayers over the past week. Share any new concerns or prayer requests and commit to praying over them in the upcoming week.

Session Recap

- If in a class, reconvene in the large group. Choose one group or a participant to recap the session highlights.
- The opening passage for this session connects praising the Lord with "forgetting not" all the beneficial things he has done. We also can praise God for not forgetting us.
- Share experiences from the Session 2 "This Week at Home," bending your will to love in difficult circumstances, praying for God to grow your love, and writing a letter to your future child pledging unconditional love.

My takeaways from this session:

_____

_____

_____

_____

_____

_____

_____

_____

_____

_____

This Week at Home

Discuss with your spouse how you can build a spiritual heritage of remembering God in your family life. You can read the Bible and pray together at regular times, show hospitality to others, and serve at your church or in your community together. Remember that your inner-workings with each other will set the tone for it all.

Decide how you will recognize God as you create fond memories in your child's life through 1) traditions like day trips to a park or beach; 2) celebrations, like birthday rituals; 3) and familiar routines, like reading together before bedtime. Your intentional choices for faith-building can impact the family's spiritual life now and become your most influential legacy.

Next Steps

- Discuss logistics related to the next time you'll meet.
- Read aloud one of the early childhood board book connections:
  All of Me That You Can't See
  To The Sea

Closing Prayer

Close your group time in prayer, thanking God for the ability to remember, and asking him to show you all how to use it in building your families' faith.

Session Four
Seek

The Lord your God is in your midst,
a mighty one who will save;
he will rejoice over you with gladness;
he will quiet you by his love;
he will exult over you with loud singing.
—Zephaniah 3:17, ESV

Opening Prayer

Ask God to meet with you and give you the desire to seek him.

Video Introduction

Video #4 – Even while God seeks us, he sets *seeking him* on the heart of humankind for its great benefit.

Session Objective

A soul must be sustained by its Source. Seeking is the steady exertion we make to affirm and grow our intimacy with God. We discover in the process that our spiritual thirst protects us from complacency, distraction, or unbelief, and develops a pattern our children will follow.

Small Group Discussion

Break into your small groups for the next three discussion topics to discuss the wisdom and benefits of seeking for parent and child.

1. Practice God's presence

As the deer pants for streams of water, so my soul pants for you, my God. My soul thirsts for God, for the living God. When can I go and meet with God?

—Psalm 42:1-2

A mind surrendered to and focused on God is seeking God's will for every action. And all the time, we are being slowly conformed to his likeness, becoming who he made us to be, according to his specific plan for our lives.

With spirits bent on seeking God, a mom and dad never run out of hope. New possibilities and spiritual discoveries are always around the corner. The unknowns of life transform into a confident Known, because we are continually in touch with our benevolent Teacher.

Seeking brings surety, a faith that understands what cannot be seen. It grows our desire to know God more, deepening our roots in Him. We withstand the storms and revel in the changing seasons. A posture of seeking will guard your child by strengthening spiritual muscles of far greater benefit than any academic or physical achievements.

And so, for the Christian life the willful focus on God's presence is our day in, day out spiritual nourishment. We don't need to do anything, but turn our minds to God and be with him. It can be done anywhere, anyplace, anytime. God meets each individual in a specially tailored way, richly blessing and encouraging the seeker.

- In Psalm 42:1-2, the psalmist passionately identifies his need as spiritual thirst. Look in the Bible for other references to thirsting for God. How "thirsty" are you? What propels your desire to go and meet with God?

- Discuss the many ways throughout the day you would benefit from turning your mind to God, absorbing his great love and acting according to his will. How will your child benefit from seeing you do this consistently in daily life?

- Tell about the most recent time your prayerful seeking resulted in a customized response from God, and how you knew it was just for you.

_____

_____

_____

_____

_____

_____

_____

_____

_____

_____

_____

_____

2. Cultivate beneficial patterns

His divine power has given us everything we need for a godly life through our knowledge of him who called us by his own glory and goodness.

—2 PETER 1:3

Reflexes and routines can either build your personal and family life with God or impede it. Beneficial patterns train us to cooperate with the Spirit.

Established habits seem to have an overwhelming advantage over our best intentions and willpower. How many New Year's resolutions putter out after the first few weeks? How many new gimmicks will we try in order to break a bad habit or establish a good one? How often do we put off going to church because we just can't seem to get into the swing of it?

We are living, breathing, walking, talking contradictions who cannot cultivate beneficial patterns in our lives until God frees us and empowers us. That's what Paul refers to as our wretched bodies being at war with our best intentions (Romans 7:24).

Fortunately, we have an Advocate, the Holy Spirit, deposited within us to guide and strengthen us for the task (John 14:25-26).

- Is there a routine that ensnares you? Is there something you need God's power to start or quit?
- What would surrendering to God's will and establishing "Christ in me" look like in your daily life (Galatians 2:20)?
- Think about your morning routine and discretionary time in the evenings. Share with your group one or two activities that build togetherness with God and in your marriage and family.

_____

_____

_____

_____

_____

_____

_____

_____

"There is not in the world a kind of life more sweet and delightful than that of a continual conversation with God."

—Brother Lawrence,
The Practice of the
Presence of God

3. Pursue fruitful knowledge

Hold on to instruction, do not let it go; guard it well, for it is your life.

—PROVERBS 4:13

> The Word of God is active and alive. Open your Bible to encounter a Person, and experience the benefits of his life-giving wisdom.

Hunger for knowledge, a pressing need to know, has been a foundation for spiritual development throughout time. On the spiritual journey, that hunger is fed by God's Word, his history with humankind as recorded in the Holy Bible.

Growing your knowledge about God will create a filter for everything you encounter. You will be positively transformed along the way "by the renewing of your mind. Then you will be able to test and approve what God's will is—his good, pleasing, and perfect will" (Romans 12:2).

As you study the Bible, consider that you are encountering a Person who desires to meet with you there. Engaging with God through his Word results in a dynamic, interactive conversation with him that permeates a soul, a marriage, and the whole of family life.

• Read aloud Hebrews 4:12 and 2 Timothy 3:16-17. Considering both of these references, what practical benefits can you draw from applying Scripture to your life?

- If you and your spouse don't currently read the Bible, what obstacles are in the way, and how could you overcome them?

- How does your marriage and family life benefit if you study the Bible on a regular basis together?

_____

_____

_____

_____

_____

_____

_____

_____

_____

_____

_____

_____

_____

_____

Small Group Wrap-Up

Close your small group time by sharing answered prayers over the past week. Share any new concerns or prayer requests and commit to praying over them in the upcoming week.

Session Recap

- If in a class, reconvene in the large group. Choose one group or a participant to recap the session highlights.

- The opening passage for this session comes from a soul deeply in need of God's presence, reflecting a life-saving hunger to seek and to meet with God.

- Share experiences from the Session 3 "This Week at Home," determining ways you will cultivate your family's spiritual heritage.

My takeaways from this session:

_____

_____

_____

_____

_____

_____

_____

_____

_____

_____

_____

This Week at Home

There's no time like the present to cultivate a beneficial pattern, right? Reading and re-reading the entire Bible in a continuous, simple, even methodical fashion is a good way to get grounded in it. Seek out one of the many Bible-in-a-year plans and commit to following it by establishing a routine, say, first thing in the morning, or at night before bedtime. Underline and copy passages that resonate with you and memorize them so they stay with you. Knowing the Bible for yourself will build your confidence and prepare you as nothing else can to answer the many curious questions your child will ask about God and the world he created.

Next Steps

- Discuss logistics related to the next time you'll meet.
- Read aloud one of the early childhood board book connections:
    Jesus Saves Me, the Knowing My God Series
    Mud Puddle Hunting Day

Closing Prayer

Close your group time in prayer, thanking God that when we seek him, we find him. Thank Jesus for coming to seek and save the lost (Luke 19:10).

Session Five
Question

With all wisdom and understanding, he made known to us the mystery of his will according to his good pleasure, which he purposed in Christ, to be put into effect when the times reach their fulfillment—to bring unity to all things in heaven and on earth under Christ.

—EPHESIANS 1:8-10

Opening Prayer

Thank God that we can take all of our questions to him and know that he will help us make meaning out of our circumstances.

Video Introduction

Video #5 – Becoming a parent often evokes deeply spiritual questions about a family's future amid uncertainties.

Session Objective

Questioning is the ability you have to spur and guide your life's growth, and a hallmark practice of earnest discipleship under Jesus. The same process plays itself over in marriage and parenting, and it is indispensable to your child's developing spiritual life.

Small Group Discussion

Break into your small groups for the next three discussion topics to discuss the benefits of questioning for growing in knowledge and truth.

1. Grapple with God

Whom have I in heaven but you?
And earth has nothing I desire besides you.
My flesh and my heart may fail,
But God is the strength of my heart
and my portion forever.
—Psalm 73:25-26

On the road to becoming more like Christ, God necessarily leads us through times that inspire questioning. In love, he shows us meaning in our frustrations, loss, and suffering.

We have a lot of questions for God, don't we? We question God's plans—the paradoxes, enigmas, and traumas involved with them. Nonbelievers ask such questions of God, too. The real paradox is that apart from God, questioning is an exercise in futility, "a chasing after the wind," as Ecclesiastes—the great book of questioning—illustrates so well.

Only God's true perspective gives our lives meaning, and so when we grapple with our questions we must do so with God. What we believe to be true about him determines the philosophies by which we operate, intentionally or not, and greatly influences our lives.

But we are not left to our own devices. God gives us illuminating writings in the books of Job, Psalms, Proverbs, and Ecclesiastes, with insights into the mysteries surrounding God's purposes and the reality of his divine attributes. These books of the Bible teach us how to reverentially wrestle with God in order to live out the faith he gives us.

- When you were growing up, was questioning God something permitted, discouraged, or encouraged?

- When in your life have you questioned God most? What resulted, and how did it impact your faith?

- God also uses questions to teach us, as Jesus often did with his disciples. Open your Bibles to Job—the oldest book in the Bible—and scan chapters 38-41. What is the essence of the questions God asked Job? What do you think about Job's response in 42:1-6?

- Young children are famously inquisitive. Your child will certainly ask you about God! How would you answer the common toddler question: Where does God live?

_____

_____

_____

_____

_____

_____

_____

_____

_____

_____

_____

_____

_____

2. Recognize the enemy

I am sending you out like sheep among wolves. Therefore be as shrewd as snakes and as innocent as doves.

—MATTHEW 10:16

> We have a powerful enemy of the soul.
> But Satan is not God. He only knows and does
> what God permits in order to achieve God's purpose
> for us and toward God's final victory over evil.

Perhaps nothing on earth is as threatening to Satan as a new spirit, fresh from the breath of God. Nothing spells promise for God's plan like a newborn child and the deep bonds created in a growing family. But Jesus says, "take heart," because his victory is everywhere (John 16).

Your new creation—a dad and mom and baby—the promise of your new family, is a major force for good in God's world. The enemy doesn't like that, but he is no match for the one who lives in you or for the prayers whispered in Jesus' name (1 John 4:4). God's Spirit is constantly at work to help us overcome.

Your marriage is a lynchpin, an outpost of promise against the devil's schemes, and it will be tested for all it is worth. Question everything. Under the pressures in this life, when your spouse snaps at you about money or says something hurtful, just see it for what it is:

a tired soul worked on by the temptations within and the dark forces without. If you feel menaced in this new phase, please recognize it is because you are being menaced (Ephesians 6:10-12).

- Review Romans 7:21-25. Name a way you have recently experienced this inner conflict of opposing wills?

- How much conscious thought do you give to the reality of spiritual warfare in your daily life?

- In Ephesians 6:10-18, Paul encourages believers to "put on the full armor of God" to equip them against the schemes of their enemy. What pieces of spiritual armor do you need to acquire or utilize for more personal victory?

_____

_____

_____

_____

_____

_____

_____

_____

_____

_____

_____

_____

_____

_____

_____

3. Tether to truth

I remember the days of long ago;
I meditate on all your works
and consider what your hands have done.
I spread out my hands to you;
I thirst for you like a parched land.
Answer me quickly, Lord;
my spirit fails.

—PSALM 143:5-7

> Having a truthful, informed understanding about God and eternity is crucial for marriages and new parents because your grasp on reality will guide the way you live and teach.

We must remain vigilant with questioning, because we live in a world where bad is called good, bondage is called freedom, and love is called hate. We see no end in sight to the perversion of basic logic and reason, and the assault on any who disagree.

Physical facts are subjected to temporary feelings. Reality is malleable. Absurdly, like the book *1984*, which George Orwell wrote in 1948, we are living in a time where truth is nonexistent because the world does not want it nor believe in it. Now, a "truth" evolves when a statement is proclaimed and repeated enough until everyone accepts it to be true.

As Christians, we must have a tether, a constant connection to truth in our lives. We are to consider the source of all that streams into our mind. "Test everything," Paul said, and truly we must (1 Thessalonians 5:21-22).

- What are some common things the Bible identifies as destructive, but that our culture calls good? What are some things the Bible identifies as good but our culture opposes?
- How has questioning in the search for truth, or the lack of questioning, shaped your view of God? What are the results?
- We all are students of someone, so listen and discern. What impact do the leaders and mentors in your life have on you? Do they lead you in truth?

_____

_____

_____

_____

_____

_____

_____

_____

_____

Small Group Wrap-Up

Close your small group time by sharing answered prayers over the past week. Share any new concerns or prayer requests and commit to praying over them in the upcoming week.

Session Recap

- If in a class, reconvene in the large group. Choose one group or a participant to recap the session highlights.

- The opening passage for this session instructs that God makes known the mystery of his will, in unity under Christ, so that we may grasp a reality and faith that make sense.

- Share experiences from the Session 4 "This Week at Home," establishing a Bible reading routine.

My takeaways from this session:

_____

_____

_____

_____

_____

_____

_____

_____

_____

_____

_____

_____

This Week at Home

List with your spouse all the questions you both have for God about your lives and your future or new child. Then list all the questions you have for each other about your marriage or future plans. Does one stand out? Pray over any lingering tension you might have about not having clear-cut answers just yet. Meet with a pastor at your church to discuss the matters troubling you. Regularly bring your questions back to God in prayer, earnestly asking him for his perspective on your circumstances.

Next Steps

- Discuss logistics related to the next time you'll meet.
- Read aloud one of the early childhood board book connections:
  Jesus Helps Me, the Knowing My God Series
  Close as a Breath

Closing Prayer

Close your group time in prayer, thanking God for the ability to question, and acknowledging his faithful answers and guidance.

Session Six

Persevere

Fear not, for I have redeemed you;
  I have called you by name, you are mine.
When you pass through the waters, I will be with you;
  and through the rivers, they shall not overwhelm you;
when you walk through fire you shall not be burned,
  and the flame shall not consume you.
For I am the Lord your God,
  the Holy One of Israel, your Savior.
    —ISAIAH 43:1-3, ESV

Opening Prayer

Ask God to help you discuss the power of persevering in a believer's life and ways you will use it in the days ahead.

Video Introduction

Video #6 – Persevering under Jesus' care permits moms and dads to overcome trials of every kind.

Session Objective

In God's design, "there is a time for everything and a season for every activity under the heavens" (Ecclesiastes 3:1). As you persevere, you give God opportunities to work in your life in unmistakable ways, to get to the other side, and to lead a peaceful family life through Jesus.

Small Group Discussion

Break into your small groups for the next three discussion topics about the necessity and potential for perseverance in your faith.

1. Stay safe in the fold

Very truly I tell you, I am the gate for the sheep. All who have come be-fore me are thieves and robbers, but the sheep have not listened to them. I am the gate; whoever enters through me will be saved. They will come in and go out, and find pasture. The thief comes only to steal and kill and destroy; I have come that they may have life, and have it to the full. I am the good shepherd.

—JOHN 10:7-11

Being part of a church that pleases God and resonates with both your spouse and your soul is vital. It is there, not in the world, where your family will find reinforcement to persevere.

Sheep find safety in their flock. Getting separated makes them afraid. The security and comfort of resting in the fold at night makes them feel safe. Safety in numbers holds true for people in the spiritual world, too.

Having fellowship and worshipping with other believers is God's idea. Jesus said, "And I tell you, you are Peter, and on this rock I will build my church, and the gates of Hades will not overcome it" (Matthew 16:18). However, it means much more than a building. It is a Presence.

The Church, with Christ at the head, is a heavenly force achieving God's plan by persevering to make disciples of all the nations. It works with amazing versatility, purpose, and creativity. Just like the parts of the human body, every aspect plays its part for the glory of God and the benefit of its members.

- Read aloud 1 Corinthians 12:12-31. Discuss why God might have created the church in this way. How could your family also function as a body?

- How do the members of a body make it stronger, more resilient in persevering?

- There are no perfect churches because there are no perfect people. The Bible gives much guidance for how believers are to relate to one another. These words are instructive for family members, too. Discuss a few that are guiding principles for you. If needed, see Galatians 6:1-6, Colossians 3:1-17, or Romans 13:8-10 as starting points.

_____

_____

_____

_____

_____

_____

_____

_____

_____

_____

_____

_____

2. Lean on the faithful

Therefore, since we are surrounded by such a great cloud of witnesses, let us throw off everything that hinders and the sin that so easily entangles. And let us run with perseverance the race marked out for us, fixing our eyes on Jesus, the pioneer and perfecter of faith. For the joy set before him he endured the Cross, scorning its shame, and sat down at the right hand of the throne of God. Consider him who endured such opposition from sinners, so that you will not grow weary and lose heart.

—HEBREWS 12:1-3

> Perseverance demonstrates love for God and others like nothing else can. Draw encouragement to persevere by studying the spiritual chronicles of others and claim them as your brothers and sisters in Christ.

While our physical lives have great variety from person to person, they have common organs and systems that make them human bodies.

The same is true of our spiritual lives. We are individually unique, yet all spirits have common functionalities that make them spirits. That's why we can draw much encouragement to persevere by studying the spiritual journeys of others. We find something intimately familiar about them.

When you study heroes of faith in the Bible, you see their struggles and their losses. You also see their eventual fruits from working cooperatively with God. When you consider that your life, your marriage, and your child are as important to God as Job's and David's and Mary's, you understand that you have the same standing with God. You have the same power to persevere—and prevail—as they and so many others have. You see how God works in many different ways to achieve his good purpose, and you remember that you are not alone.

- Which Bible figures stand out to you? Think about the struggles they faced and how those very hardships later led to their victorious faith.

- Who else in your life is a hero of faith to you and why?

- Take time to consider specific trials you have had, and reflect on the character-shaping benefits that you reaped. In what ways did God encourage you?

3. Keep it simple

Come to me, all you who are weary and burdened, and I will give you rest. Take my yoke upon you and learn from me, for I am gentle and humble in heart, and you will find rest for your souls. For my yoke is easy, and my burden is light.

—MATTHEW 11:28-30

> Jesus introduced an entirely new perspective by teaching beyond the letter of the law to the spirit of it. His often-repeated lesson was that the inner state of a person matters more than anything else.

Seasons of life-change, and even those of abundance, can easily distract or consume all of your energy. Life pulls you in many directions with the demands of young children, work pressures, and so many different distractions that can fritter away time.

But a life intentionally ordered around matters of the spirit brings reality into focus from the core. There, Jesus offers a sublimely simple life with him. We find freedom from unnamed pressure or unfruitful thinking that bogs us down and zaps our strength. We find focus and purpose. The yoke is sweeter. The burden is indeed lighter.

Even though you cannot see, touch, or hear Jesus in the physical way, you can choose to take on his yoke and rest with him. You can love the things Jesus loves. Remember the things he remembers. Seek the things he seeks. Question the things he questions. And persevere for all that he perseveres.

With Jesus, the Christian life is marked by service, sacrifice, and suffering that sculpt and refine the soul. Day by day you will become more like him. As you do, you'll find rest. Your marriage will experience God's presence and peace, and your child will be blessed.

- Read aloud the account of Martha and Mary in Luke 10:38-42. External factors still had a strong hold on Martha, while Mary already recognized that time with Jesus was most important. Works in progress that we are, where does your spiritual life fall on the spectrum? What did Jesus confirm by his response?

- A common thread running throughout the Old Testament is, "wait for the Lord; be patient and wait." After he came, the imperative became, "Don't give up!" Stand firm. All the New Testament writers stress perseverance, and Jesus himself urges it. Use your memory or concordance to look up and share examples of perseverance in the Bible.

- Read aloud 2 Corinthians 4:16-18. How does this strengthen you for the days ahead?

_____

_____

_____

_____

_____

_____

Small Group Wrap-Up

Permit a few extra minutes to talk about what these six sessions have meant to you. Talk about what the future holds, and then close in prayer for the spiritual future of your families.

Session Recap

- If in a class, reconvene in the large group. Choose one group or a participant to recap the session highlights.

- The opening passage for this session on Perseverance highlights the trials of life that are overcome by an all-powerful and benevolent God.

- Share experiences from the Session 5 "This Week at Home," listing and praying over lingering questions you have about God, faith, or your family.

My takeaways from this session:

_____

_____

_____

_____

_____

_____

_____

_____

_____

_____

_____

This Week at Home

Observe how your spiritual abilities to Love, Remember, Seek, Question, and Persevere help you through your days. Spend time with your spouse to thumb through the Group Study and your notes. Discuss the things that struck you most, which you listed in take-aways. Decide how they will inform your family's developing faith and determine your lifestyles starting today.

Next Steps

- Discuss ways your group or class can stay in touch or continue meeting on a regular basis.
- Read aloud one of the early childhood board book connections:
  Jesus Invites Me, the Knowing My God Series
  Little Seed: A Life

Closing Prayer

Close your group time in prayer, praising God for his promise to help you through trials and see you to the other side. Give thanks for the class time together and pray for his blessing on the newly developing families and the young souls he has made.

Helpful Resources

Large and Small Group Guidelines

Whether you are part of a small group that has been together for a while, or this is your first time in a Bible study class or small group setting, you are striking out into something new: the unknowns of parenting and your new child.

Regardless of your backgrounds, you will have common ground as part of this unique study that explores innate spiritual abilities, which are vital for the spiritual care and nurturing of your growing family.

Here are some best practices to keep in mind during your time together:

- All group and small group discussions are to be grounded in trust, confidentiality, and love.

- Be mindful of the schedule and agree to move larger discussions or off-topic questions to the side. Participants are always welcome to do further study outside of the class.

- As individuals, strive for a balance of not speaking too much or contributing too little. Openness and sharing of all leads to a great variety of perspectives and new understandings.

- Don't worry if sharing or talking in a group doesn't come naturally to you. Others will understand and give you the space needed to warm up to it.

- Resist the temptation to talk while another is talking. Listening is a great asset in any class, and a prime parenting skill to develop.

- Consider forming new parent small groups after this course so that you can apply Scripture studies to the challenges you will likely have in common.

Know that meeting regularly with other parents who are beginning their spiritual journey with young children will be a valuable investment of your time.

Organizer Leadership Tips

- This material is suitable for couples who are not yet expecting, are currently expecting, or already have young children. You might consider offering nursery or childcare so all such parents can attend.

- Allow one-and-a-half to two hours per session. The course is ideal for Sunday mornings or evenings after work. You might also host a Saturday workshop or weekend retreat with all six sessions—three in the morning and three in the afternoon with a lunch break in between.

- The sessions have three parts:
    1. Large group welcome, video introduction, opening prayer (10 minutes)
    2. Small group breakouts to discuss three applications (45-60 minutes)
    3. Reconvene large groups for a recap, review of what to do at home during the week, other next steps, board book reading, closing prayer (10 minutes)

- Each session concludes with two board book connections, and suggests choosing one to read aloud. These optional books complement the session topics and inspire expecting or new parents to read to their children from birth, which is vital for cognitive, emotional, and spiritual development. Parents will benefit from these books, too—as they reinforce the biblical content of the Newborn Promise Project. Bundles are available at grahamblanchard.com or contact your local Christian retailer.

- Consider broadening the class promotion beyond your regular channels. Church pre-schools have many seeking or nonbelieving families. Reach out to them for this accessible study. They might be spiritually struggling, and it could be just the lifesaver they need.

- You could partner with a local Christian retailer who might have meeting space, offer special discounts or incentives, or co-promote your class. They would welcome the opportunity to get to know your community.

- Organize a leadership team to serve as mentors for the class, by involving couples who are in the next life stage with somewhat older children. These trailblazers are not so far ahead from the new parents that they cannot relate to today's challenges, and they offer the "I've just been there and lived through it" kind of support. These couples can lead the small group breakouts and even become ongoing mentors to their participants.

- Encourage the small groups to continue meeting or to start a new small group to support their family in the ages and stages ahead.

- Host a Parent Dedication wrap-up celebration at the end of the last session or on a subsequent meeting of your organization or congregation. This brief ceremony would include a prayer certificate (downloadable from www.grahamblanchard.com), and a small gift from your organization if budget allows.

- Recognize the couples' work and affirm their commitment to building and growing together in faith. Close with a laying on the hands, as a commission (Acts 13:3), or simply by praying, and offering the promise to support and pray for them in the years ahead.

- Encourage your participants to tune into the Newborn Promise

Podcast and free app for ongoing support, shared experiences, and tips.

Learn about the experiences of other group or class leaders at grahamblanchard.com.

What is Your Faith Style?

All Christians have preferences for living out their faith. For example, some find the greatest encouragement in a group study, others in quite time reading. Some enjoy walking in nature for prayer, others prefer to be in the sanctity of a church building.

All of these are strengths! But relying exclusively on one or two aspects of faith, can lead to a life that is spiritually limited, not living up to the potential that Jesus offers in order for us to become more like him.

What's more, the faith style of parents greatly influences how they spiritually parent their children.

Graham Blanchard's Learn, Absorb, Praise, & Connect framework for grownups is designed to help you round out your spiritual life and fully grow in faith. We've designed a 12-question quiz to assess your dominant faith style. It's free at www.grahamblanchard.com. Take it today and find out nine easy ways to avoid your blindsides, plus a few more tips that play to your strengths.

From the Authors

Not long after introducing the first of its kind Learn, Absorb & Praise™ Christian board book collection for children ages 0 to 7, we recognized a gap in support for their moms and dads, too, as they step into entirely new roles as parents and enter a new phase in marriage and their individual development.

We devoted the next year to talking with parents, pastors, and teachers about how to best guide expecting and new parents in this major life transition—both its challenges and its divinely appointed potential. We prayed a lot.

For two more years, we continued as students. We studied what the Bible had to say about our relationship with God and with each other. There, we immersed in the experiences of others and listened to God's instruction. We reflected on our own marriages and parenting experiences, and God's work through them.

Often during the course of this work, we were in the midst of the very challenges we were writing about. We juggled schedules, went through parenting crises with our children, and worked among laundry baskets and other routines of daily life. As of this writing, our extended team has brought five new lives into the world, experienced miscarriage, infertility, problem pregnancy, sent kids to college, moved to new cities, and experienced unsolvable medical issues and the death of parents. Our family lives are just like yours.

Along the way, the Newborn Promise Project kept us focused on our loving God. We have all been changed by the process, and we pray that you will be changed by it, too. We will always be students with you, on this great adventure of everlasting life together.

—*Callie Grant, Audra Haney, Charissa Kolar, August 2017*

Working for publishers like Scholastic and Dorling Kindersley, Callie developed creative educational content to build children's literacy and learning skills. It wasn't until she had a child of her own that she appreciated how important reading from birth is—for cognitive, emotional, and spiritual development. In 2011, she launched Graham Blanchard to create Christian board books and parenting resources for new families growing up in God. Callie lives in Austin, Texas, with her husband, Michael, and their daughter.

Audra has written and produced quality Christian broadcast content for a wide range of audiences across the globe. But after welcoming her first child in 2014 and navigating the new (and sometimes choppy) waters of parenting, Audra decided to combine her media-life and mom-life to reach out to her favorite audience yet: expecting and new parents. Audra co-produces and hosts the Newborn Promise Podcast. She lives in Knoxville, Tennessee, with her husband, Cory, a missions pastor, and their two daughters.

Charissa joined the original start-up team at Graham Blanchard as an editorial advisor for child and parent content. Today, she continues program development and co-produces the Newborn Promise Podcast. Charissa also combines her passion for the spiritual development of families with her extensive communications background to write about the adventures—and often humorous mishaps—of parenting two energetic boys alongside her husband, Rob. Her family lives in the San Francisco East Bay Area.

The Newborn Promise Project Collection

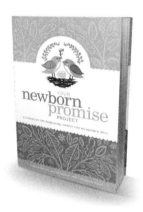

Individual and Couple Study

For deeper personal study, the Primer aligns with the Group Study sessions Love, Remember, Seek, Question, and Persevere. It also discusses five Bible-based newborn facts of life about children and includes Learn, Absorb, Praise, and Connect activities for individuals and couples to intimately assess and plan for building their family's faith.

Your Newborn Promise Project: A Christian Pre-Parenting Primer for Husband & Wife
Paperback, $14.99, 6x9, 176 pages
ISBN 9780989794985

Newborn Promise Podcast

Join author Audra Haney and friends each week to navigate your growing family's spiritual life with the support of other parents well-regarded in their fields. Series cover topics from Building Your Family to After the Baby Arrives, with first-hand accounts that will guide and inspire the spiritual vitality of families in transition. Available at grahamblanchard.com, through the Newborn Promise Project App, and on Google Play and iTunes.

Coloring and Activity Book

Young children can start thinking about their own Newborn Promise and what life in the Spirit means for them. Led by the Knowing My God series Soul Mates, your child will color, imagine, draw, write, solve, and dream their way through creative applications of the grown-up Primer. For ages 4 & up.

Your Newborn Promise Project Wings
Paperback, $6.99, 8.5 x 11 inches, 32 pages
ISBN 9780692850336

The Newborn Promise
Project Collection

"If people take this to heart they will have saved thousands of dollars
they would have spent in counseling for themselves and for their kids. I'm not joking.
This is really powerful. It is like going on a soul journey with Jesus."

—Matt Warner, Campus Pastor, Cornerstone Fellowship, Danville, CA

Your Newborn Promise True Story Videos

FREE! With Primer or Group Study book purchase. Use coupon code NPPGSC
at www.grahamblanchard.com to download artfully produced videos featur-
ing couples who share their experiences as new parents building faith.

Newborn Promise App

Expecting and new parents have automatic access to ideas, inspiration,
and podcast updates through a beautiful interface available on all devices.

What is Your Faith Style?

Take the quiz at grahamblanchard.com and find out why it matters.

The first years of a child's life are the most important time for cognitive, social, and emotional development, and are essential for establishing a life-long love for Jesus. The spiritual abilities explored in the Newborn Promise parenting resources—**Love**, **Remember**, **Seek**, **Question**, **Persevere**— naturally correlate with the basic Biblical concepts in our board books. Reading them together from the start strengthens family ties as infant, mom, and dad build and grow together in their faith.

Love

Created in God's Image

Because we are created in God's image, love creates a spiritual bond, not a physical one. Family bonds are primarily spiritual unions of love. The Bible describes love best. Look closely at what God says about love: *Jesus Shows Me*, the Knowing My God series (ISBN 9780985409036) and *Your Core* (ISBN 9780985409050).

Remember

A Friend to Faith

When we are rooted and established in Jesus, time is a friend to faith. As we grow, we carry memories of how God has revealed himself in our personal lives and in the human history of the Bible. The family of God creates loving memories with him: *All of Me That You Can't See* (ISBN 9780985409043) and *To The Sea* (ISBN 9780989794947).

Board book format fits small hands, 18-24 pages, $8.99 each

Seek

The Protecting Thirst

A soul must be nurtured by its Source. Seeking is the steady effort we make to grow in closeness with God. We discover along the way that our spiritual thirst protects us, and helps develop a lifetime pattern of finding: *Jesus Saves Me*, the Knowing My God series (ISBN 9780985409029) and *Mud Puddle Hunting Day* (ISBN 9780985409005).

Question

Blessed By Curiosity

Questioning is the ability we have to spur and guide our life's growth. The hunger to know is a hallmark practice of earnest disciple-ship under Jesus, and it is indispensable to a developing spiritual life with him: *Jesus Helps Me*, the Knowing My God series (ISBN 9780989794954) and *Close as a Breath* (ISBN 9780985409067).

Persevere

A Season for All

In God's design, "there is a time for every-thing and a season for every activity under the heavens." As you persevere, he works in your life in unmistakable ways, to achieve your purpose in peace with Jesus: *Jesus Invites Me*, the Knowing My God series (ISBN: 9780985409012) and *Little Seed: A Life* (ISBN: 9780985409074).

Early Childhood Books With Newborn Promise

What's so great about board books? Everything going on inside! Small, sturdy board books pack a lot of punch with their beautiful pictures and thoughtfully chosen words. That's why parents love our books and learn from them, too. Reading aloud together becomes a treasured tradition that deepens family ties.

small size for little hands

A sample spread from: Jesus Shows Me, Knowing My God Series

DISCUSS full page, color photos that delight, inspire, teach

SHARE a passage from Jesus

CONNECT Scripture to life

sturdy pages built to last

A sample spread from: All of Me That You Can't See

UNDERSTAND the importance of a strong spiritual life

APPLY the principles to real-life situations

colorful vibrant artwork

A sample spread from: Little Seed: A Life

EXPERIENCE the beauty of nature and growth

LEARN facts about science

Early Childhood Books With Newborn Promise

"The artwork is amazing, the words are biblical, and the conversations that these books spur are a huge help to parents. So, Learn, Absorb & Praise—true for kids and parents."

—Brad Thomas, Lead Pastor, Austin Ridge Bible Church, Austin, TX

Newborn Promise Parent Tips

Extend your family's experience with the Learn, Absorb & Praise™ board book collection to practice the presence of God in daily life. These simple ideas connect themes from the board books with the Newborn Promise Project, reinforcing a parent's own spiritual growth, too. Available as a free download.